The Coming of the English

The End of Roman London

In AD 410 the cities or 'states' of Roman Britain were advised by the Emperor Honorius to take their own measures for protection against barbarian raids; no fresh troops could be sent to their aid from Rome, the hard-pressed imperial capital. Perhaps in recognition of a *fait accompli,* but with no intention that the situation should be permanent, Rome accepted the independence of Britain. So perforce did the inhabitants, most of them native Britons, Romanized Celts, though with a sprinkling of administrators and settlers from elsewhere in the empire. What measures the British took for the protection of such cities as London are not clear. London's walls were no doubt in good condition, having been strengthened with towers on the east and a new wall on the river front within the last 60 years. Yet the area within them was not densely populated. Layers of dark earth overlying earlier Roman buildings on a number of sites excavated in the city suggest that parts of the walled enclosure had long been used as farmland or lain waste.

The threat to Britain was from the Picts from north of Hadrian's Wall, the Irish from the west, and the Saxons and related German tribes raiding across the North Sea. To face them the Roman authorities had employed mercenaries in addition to their regular troops; many of them were themselves from Germany, some no doubt Saxons. Such mercenary troops, *foederati,* were granted land, which they settled with their families, in return for their service. At Mucking, in Essex, on a

Brooch of gilded silver, 6th-century. This fine piece of jewellery fastened the cloak of a woman who was buried in the Saxon cemetery at Mitcham.

hilltop overlooking a great bend in the Thames, where any ship-borne force moving upriver could be seen in good time, excavations have revealed a village of Saxon settlers which existed in the early 5th century, perhaps guarding the river route towards London. On the far side of the city, at Mitcham, Surrey, burials have been found indicating the presence of another Saxon settlement, and though most of the burials are later, early objects found in some of the graves suggest that a village already existed here by, or shortly after, AD 400; the same may be true of other sites, around Croydon. These could be deliberate plantations of federate troops guarding the south and south-west approaches to the Roman city.

The newly independent local British authorities seem to have continued Roman policy, with disastrous results, for in the middle of the 5th century the mercenaries mutinied. In Kent, under the leadership of Hengist, they defeated a force of their former British masters at *Crecganford* (perhaps Crayford) in 457. The English chronicler who, much later, recorded the tradition of this event, wrote that the British fled to London. London could certainly have served as a centre of resistance, but there is no evidence that it did. Archaeology indicates that the Roman way of life continued in London into the 5th century; the lack of Saxon burials of this period in an area north of the city or anywhere close to it has been thought to indicate the presence of an authority strong enough to keep Saxons, mercenaries and raiders, at a distance, on the perimeter of a British enclave. Yet with the withdrawal of central control from Rome and the collapse of overseas trade the dual functions of London, as the administrative centre of one of the provinces into which late Roman Britain had been divided and as an international port, ceased. By 457 there may have been few inhabitants, and little else worth defending — or attacking. There is no account of a siege or battle; London quietly disappears from the historical record.

Anglo-Saxon Settlers

The earliest English historian, Bede, writing in about 730, said that the newcomers, ancestors of the English, were Angles and Saxons from north-west Germany and Jutes from Jutland, the

Above: Excavations at Milk Street, in the City, revealed a thick layer of dark agricultural soil overlying the remains of 2nd-century Roman buildings.

Left: A bronze buckle of late Roman type, from Smithfield. Such equipment was issued to German mercenaries in the Roman army.

Below: Pottery cup, *c.* AD 400, from the Mitcham cemetery.

Right: Skeleton of a woman buried at Mitcham. Her clothing was fastened by a long pin and a circular brooch; she had a belt with bronze fittings, and a small iron knife.

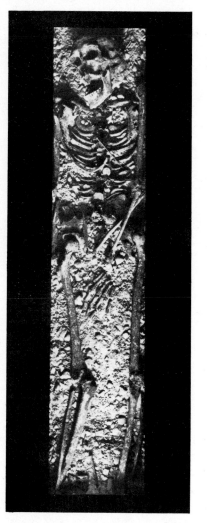

Angles settling in the north, the midlands and East Anglia, the Saxons in the areas later called Wessex, Sussex and Essex, and the Jutes chiefly in Kent. Modern archaeologists, studying their culture — their pottery, their jewellery, their burial customs — and that of their continental contemporaries, reveal a more complex picture. The settlers, 'Anglo-Saxons', to use the modern term, were small, loosely-combined groups of distinct but related peoples from Germany and the North Sea coasts. After the mercenaries came further raiders and invaders, moving inland by different routes, sometimes against stiff opposition, sometimes perhaps facing very little co-ordinated resistance.

Their advance was slow, and the British long remembered the great battle at 'Badon Hill', somewhere in the West Country soon after 500, when, led according to one tradition by a general called Arthur, they inflicted a resounding defeat on the Anglo-Saxons, stopping and indeed reversing their progress for some 50 years. Yet by the late 6th century eastern Britain was in Anglo-Saxon hands; their war-bands were coalescing into small independent, often warring, but stable kingdoms.

Not all the British could have fled to the west or (as some did) overseas to Brittany; not all died of plague or in war. Some must have remained alongside the new settlers, some been enslaved. Anglo-Saxon men may have taken British wives. Yet they learnt little from their predecessors. The Anglo-Saxons had no use for the Roman towns with their great buildings of stone and brick. Their hand-made pots replaced the factory products of the Roman world. In eastern Britain both the native British language and Latin, the official language of the empire, vanished, as did literacy. The newcomers were pagans, who brought with them their own beliefs and their own gods, of whose memory little survives apart from the names preserved in our days of the week — Tiw, Woden, Thunor and Frig, and the names of some sacred places, such as Thundersley ('Thunor's grove') in Essex and Harrow ('shrine' or 'holy place') in Middlesex.

Few of the homesteads and villages of these early settlers have been excavated. At Mucking, for example, and West Stow (Suffolk) there were groups of small huts, their floors dug below ground level, and occasional larger timber-built halls. More frequently recognized than the ephemeral remains of these farming settlements have been their burial grounds, and since (in areas where burial rather than cremation was customary) the dead were buried with things they were thought to need in the afterlife, their graves can tell much about their lives. With a man were placed his weapons — for even a farmer was expected to fight to defend his land and his lord — a spear, a wooden shield with an iron boss,

Below: **Anglo-Saxon spears, sword and iron shield-boss.**

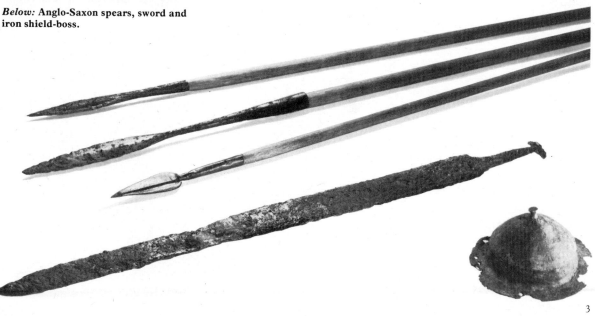

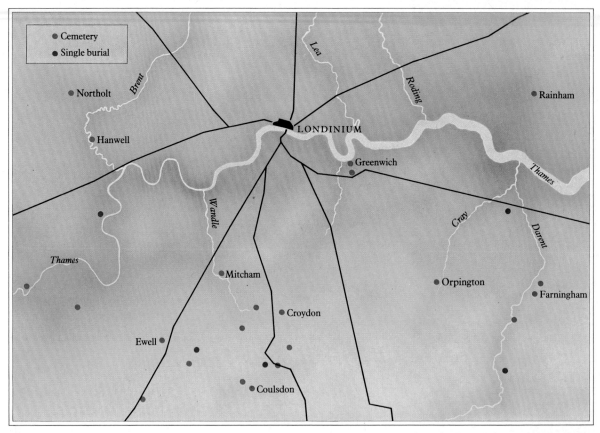

Londinium

Cemetery
Single burial

Northolt
Rainham
Hanwell
Greenwich
Thames
Mitcham
Orpington
Farningham
Croydon
Ewell
Coulsdon

Rivers labelled: Brent, Lea, Roding, Thames, Wandle, Cray, Darent

Pagan Saxon cemeteries discovered in the London area give some indication of the sites of settlements, avoiding the Roman city with its network of roads.

Right: **Glass beaker from one of the earlier, 5th-century, burials at Mitcham.**

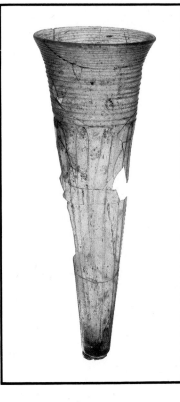

sometimes a sword; with a woman, her household utensils and jewellery; with both the brooches that fastened their clothing, and occasional valuable imports from the continent such as glass vessels, sometimes no doubt heirlooms. As well as at Mitcham, Saxon burials are recorded from the London area at Greenwich, around Croydon, Ewell, Hanwell and elsewhere; the settlements to which these cemeteries belong remain unrecognized.

The Fate of the City

Though the surviving Roman cities of Britain seem to have clung to the Roman life-style long after 410 there is little, if any, evidence for continuity of urban life from Roman into Anglo-Saxon times. In London a single 5th-century Saxon brooch was found among the fallen roof tiles of a Roman house excavated near Billingsgate, a house still occupied in the early part of the same century; it need represent no more than the presence of one woman who lost her brooch while scavenging among the ruins of the Roman city — ruins that resulted not from war but from simple neglect and decay. Archaeologically London in the later 5th and 6th centuries remains a virtual blank.

The city walls and the remains of many buildings still stood, as they did centuries later. But the self-sufficient Saxon settlers had no use for the centralized authority and bureaucracy which a city represented, and perhaps were in some awe of its buildings. A later Anglo-Saxon poet characterized the ruins of a Roman town as 'the work of giants'. It is likely that a few people lived on among 'the work of giants' in London, farming in the open areas — perhaps of British descent, perhaps Saxon; so far archaeology cannot confirm it. As an urban centre, however, London did not exist. *Londinium*, the Roman city, had died; *Lundenwic*, the Saxon market-town, had yet to be born.

Missionaries and Merchants

Kent and the Franks

By the end of the 6th century most of what is now England was occupied by small Anglo-Saxon kingdoms. Beyond them were the kingdoms of the British, descendants of the citizens of the Roman province, from Strathclyde in the north to the West Welsh of Cornwall, kingdoms little different from those of their English enemies — though nominally at least Christian. The kings of the more settled Anglo-Saxon realms in the southeast — East Angles, Mercians, East, South and West Saxons — recognized the primacy of one king, Ethelbert of Kent. The richest and longest-settled region, favoured by its position, Kent had close links with the more advanced Germanic kingdoms of Europe, where the Franks, conquerors of the Roman provinces of Germany and Gaul, had, unlike their relatives in Britain, taken over something of the culture (including the Christian religion) and technology of those areas. Thus the industrial region around the Rhine continued to work, producing for example fine glass vessels and wheel-turned pottery, some of which found its way to Britain, perhaps in trade, perhaps as gifts between kings and nobles.

In the 580s Ethelbert of Kent contracted a political marriage with Bertha, daughter of Charibert the Christian king of the Franks of Paris. With her his new wife brought her chaplain, and in time Ethelbert was persuaded to receive Christian missionaries to his kingdom — no doubt recognizing the practical advantages of bringing England into line with the rest of Europe as much as the spiritual benefits of the new religion. Sent from Rome by Pope Gregory a mission led by Augustine landed in Thanet in 597 and preached before Ethelbert and his assembled court. In time Ethelbert and many of his people became Christians, and Augustine was allowed to establish a church at the old Roman city of Canterbury and to build or restore others; in 601 Pope Gregory appointed Augustine first archbishop to the southern English. The Pope's original intention was that as the conversion of the English proceeded a number of bishops would be established under two archbishops based at the Roman provincial capitals of London and York; the authority of Ethelbert, the reputation of Augustine and later setbacks in the conversion determined that the southern archbishopric should remain at Canterbury rather than being transferred to London.

St Paul's Cathedral

London lay in the territory of the East Saxons, whose king, Saeberht, was Ethelbert's nephew and accepted him as overlord. Under Ethelbert's influence, Saeberht agreed to receive missionaries,

Glass cup and two wheel-turned pots of 6th- or early 7th-century date. Found in the City, they were imported from Germany or northern France.

and to accept the appointment of a bishop for his people, Mellitus, one of a second group who had joined Augustine's mission. However, it was Ethelbert who in 604, according to Bede, built a church in London, dedicated to St Paul, to serve as Mellitus' cathedral. Nothing is known of this first St Paul's, which presumably stood like the later cathedral on the city's prominent western hill. It may have resembled the churches built in this period in Kent, of which remains are known in Canterbury, Rochester and elsewhere; of stone, small — about 70 or 80 feet (20-25m) long — with an apsidal (round) east end, and side chapels. However, Mellitus had himself brought advice from the Pope to the missionaries in England that where possible they should reconsecrate pagan Anglo-Saxon temples for Christian use, taking advantage of existing veneration for such buildings, and it is possible that Mellitus' church was a converted East Saxon shrine, or stood on the site of one.

Bede called London the 'metropolis' of the East Saxons. However, he was writing with hindsight a century and a quarter later, and archaeology provides no picture of the size and status of this 'metropolis' in 604. It may have already served as a local trading centre, with occasional markets or fairs. The few finds from the city of Frankish glass and pottery of this period may indicate the beginnings of trade with the continent, or merely the presence of the East Saxon royal court with its links with the Franks through Kent. Saeberht's court, like that of all Anglo-Saxon kings, would have been nomadic. He could govern his essentially rural kingdom from any one of a number of royal houses and estates; presumably there was such a centre — Bede seems to imply it was the chief one — in London. Yet there need have been little more than existed at this period at the Northumbrian royal site that has been excavated at Yeavering (Northumberland): a number of timber-built halls and associated buildings, a fort, an 'amphitheatre' for public assemblies and a temple. In London the Roman city walls, more particularly perhaps the walls of the Roman fort in the north-west corner of the city, would provide the necessary fortification; the other buildings would perhaps leave little archaeological trace. If Saeberht had an occasional residence of this type in

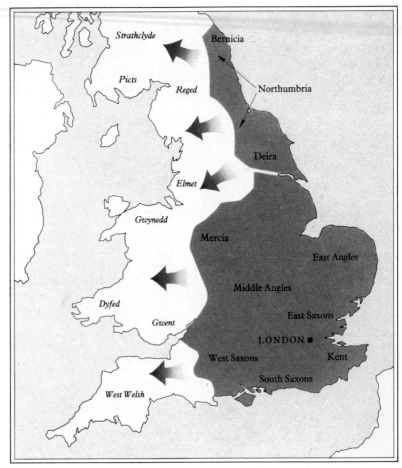

Above: **Britain *c.* AD 600. The still-expanding Anglo-Saxon kingdoms occupied the eastern part of the country; those south of Northumbria accepted Ethelbert of Kent as overlord.**

Below: **St Alban's, Wood Street. Excavations on the site of this City church revealed the foundations of the little Saxon church.**

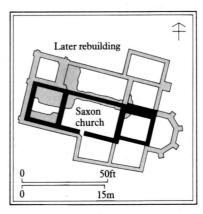

London, the permanent population of the 'metropolis', in the absence of the king and his followers, may have been at most a few hundred.

The conversion of the East Saxons was only superficial. On the death of Saeberht his people reverted to paganism and Bishop Mellitus fled from London. Though Ethelbert's death in 616 had created a similarly dangerous situation for the Christian missionaries in Kent, the Christian community survived in Canterbury, and after a year in exile its bishop returned to the other Kentish cathedral at Rochester; but the East Saxons never accepted Mellitus back in London.

Lundenwic

The setback to Christianity was only temporary. New missionaries came; by the mid 7th century the Northumbrians, the Mercians, the West Saxons, even the once recalcitrant East Saxons became Christian. The fate of London in this period is again uncertain. Bede, writing in about 730, called it an *emporium*, 'a market for many peoples coming by land and sea'. The presence of the cathedral and the advantages of London's position, close to the borders of a number of kingdoms and at a convenient meeting point of land- and sea-routes, seem to have led to its growing status and, no doubt, growing population as trade revived in more settled conditions. Gold

All Hallows by the Tower. This arch, built partly of tiles from a demolished Roman building, probably led from the body of the original church into a side-chapel.

coins were being struck by the 650s, the first English coins, imitating those of the Franks; some were presumably minted in London, for they are inscribed LONDUNIU — Canterbury was the only other town similarly honoured. Silver coins, more useful for everyday purchases, soon followed.

By the 680s men of Kent were trading in London, required by their own laws to report their dealings to their king's representative in the town; the laws refer to London as *Lundenwic* — the *-wic* ending indicates a market town or port. London remained nominally East Saxon, but the kings of Mercia had replaced those of Kent as overlords of southern England and perhaps on this basis controlled London; in the 660s it was a Mercian king who appointed the bishop of London — Bishop Wine, who paid for the appointment.

In 675 a new bishop was consecrated in succession to Wine: Erkenwald, later known as 'the Light of London', whose reputation for piety and the miracles that surrounded him in life and death led to his canonization. His shrine in St Paul's became a place of pilgrimage, still to be seen in the medieval cathedral until its destruction in 1666. Erkenwald founded a monastery at Chertsey (Surrey) and a nunnery at Barking (Essex); All Hallows by the Tower in London seems to have been founded as a daughter-church of Barking Abbey, and part of the Anglo-Saxon church there survives incorporated into the later building.

Mercian London

Other churches may have been built at this period in London. There was a later tradition that King Offa of Mercia (757-796) had a palace in the north-west corner of the town, and that the church of St Alban's Wood Street was his chapel. Certainly throughout the 8th century the area of London and Middlesex was firmly controlled by the kings of Mercia. They confirmed grants of land in the area, perhaps founded to the west of London the church which was to develop into the great medieval abbey of Westminster, and collected customs duties on ships coming to the port of London; London's trade was sufficient to provide a source of royal revenue. In 790 and 811 Mercian royal councils met in London, then described as 'a most renowned place and royal town'.

Of the Mercian kings Offa was the greatest. Overlord over all the kings of southern England, he called himself 'King of the English', and built the mighty dyke that bears his name to mark and guard the western frontier with the British of Wales. He negotiated as an equal with the Frankish emperor Charlemagne; some of their negotiations concerned trade between their two countries, and the export of English cloth, later so important as a source of national wealth, received special consideration. But there was a price to pay for growing trade and prosperity.

The Vikings

The Great Army

At the end of the 8th century *vikings*, sea-raiders from Scandinavia, began attacking the open coasts of England, plundering settlements, towns and monasteries. Their swift seaworthy ships carried them far inland along English rivers; in 842 there was 'great slaughter' at London and Rochester and in 851 a force of 350 viking ships stormed London and Canterbury. The towns of southern England had in 250 years grown in population and wealth to provide tempting targets for large-scale piracy.

At first the raiders came only in summer, but by the 850s they were regularly camping for the winter on English soil. In 865 a 'great army' of Danes gathered in East Anglia, and in a series of annual campaigns, spending each winter in a strongly-held town, they won control of northern and eastern England, destroying the Anglo-Saxon kingdoms. In 871-2 they wintered in London; nothing is known of the fate of the town or its population, nor whether the Danes left behind an occupying force when they moved on at the beginning of the next campaigning season. Mercia collapsed, its king fled. The Danes began to settle the lands they had conquered.

In 877 Wessex was invaded, the West Saxon king, Alfred, driven into hiding. In 878, however, Alfred led his troops to victory over the Danes and made peace with them. The peace did not last, and further hard fighting followed before in 886 Alfred occupied London. A treaty between Alfred and the Danish leader Guthrum confirmed Danish authority over the *Danelaw*, its boundary drawn along the Thames and up the River Lea east of London.

8

Alfred's London

Perhaps to commemorate his occupation of London Alfred issued a series of fine silver pennies bearing the monogram LONDONIA. He placed the city in the charge of Ealdorman (Earl) Aethelred, ruler of what was left of Mercia, who had accepted his supremacy, and began a programme for the resettlement and fortification of the town. A new grid of streets seems to have been laid out, ignoring the former Roman street-pattern. Grants of land, with trading privileges, at 'Aethelred's Hithe' — the port area later known as Queenhithe — were made to two bishops; similar grants may have been made to other leading nobles. What work was carried out on the defences is unknown; a stockade revealed by excavation on the shore near Billingsgate may represent an attempt to fortify the vulnerable wharves.

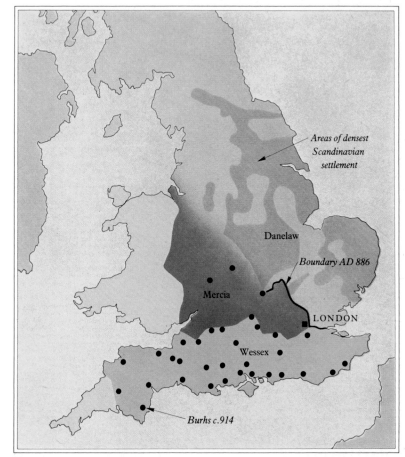

Areas of densest Scandinavian settlement

Danelaw

Boundary AD 886

Mercia

LONDON

Wessex

Burhs c.914

Above: Silver penny minted in the reign of Alfred, with on one side a monogram made up of the letters of LONDONIA — London.

Below: The Gokstad ship. Preserved in the Viking Ship Museum, Oslo, this 9th-century Norwegian ship is the sort of sea-going craft used by the viking raiders.

Left: In 886 King Alfred and the Dane Guthrum agreed on the boundary separating the 'Danelaw', where the prevelance of place-names of Scandinavian origin shows the presence of the viking invaders, from English territory, defended by fortified *burhs*.

9

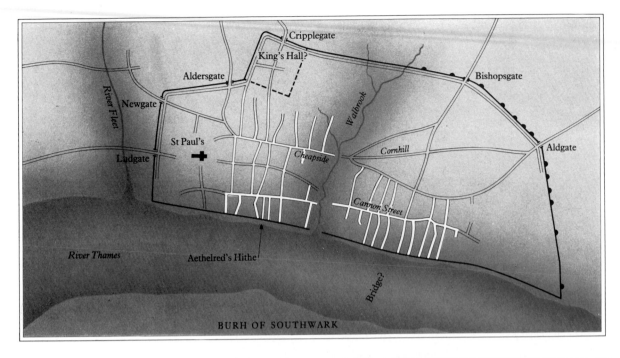

BURH OF SOUTHWARK

Alfred's London. Some documentary and archaeological evidence suggests that part of London's medieval street pattern was deliberately laid out at the end of the 9th-century, as in other Anglo-Saxon towns such as Winchester.

Right: **Stakes hammered into the foreshore near London Bridge may have been intended to prevent a landing by enemy ships.**

Throughout their territory Alfred and his successors organized a defensive system of forts and fortified towns, some new, some restored Roman walled cities or even prehistoric hill-forts. In a contemporary list of these *burhs* ('boroughs') London does not appear; Southwark does, for the first time, protecting the southern approach to the river-crossing, and together with London guarding the river itself. The fortification and defence of London and Southwark would have been the responsibility of their inhabitants and those of the surrounding area, and Alfred's planned resettlement must have proceeded rapidly, for in 893 a force of Londoners joined an English army which captured a Danish fort at Benfleet (Essex), and two years later played a major part in an attack on a similar fort on the River Lea. In later years London was to be central to the defence of southern England.

Late Saxon London

London and the King

In 911 Aethelred of Mercia died and King Edward, Alfred's son and successor, took full possession of London 'and the lands that belonged to it'. A campaign began to win back the territory ceded to the Danes, and when in 918 Aethelred's widow died and Edward was accepted as ruler by the Mercians he was sole king of a single and expanding kingdom of England. His son Athelstan was crowned at Kingston in 925; within two years he had conquered the last of the Scandinavian kingdoms in the north-east and received the surrender of the kings of Scotland and Wales. On his coins he claimed the title 'King of All Britain'.

Some of Athelstan's legislation reflects the importance of London during his reign. The issue of royal coinage was strictly controlled; though it was minted in many towns the number of moneyers in each was to be limited. London was allowed eight, more than any other, but it was approached closely by Winchester and Canterbury. It did not yet have the pre-eminence over other towns it was to achieve later, and was far from being a capital. Athelstan and his successors still issued their laws and summoned their councils at any place that was convenient. Presumably they had a palace in London, probably where legend placed that of King Offa, between Aldermanbury and Cripplegate, defended by the walls of the old Roman fort.

London was governed for the king by his *portreeve*, his 'town-agent' responsible chiefly for collecting the royal taxes and

Sites in the City where Saxon or Norman wooden buildings have been revealed by excavation.

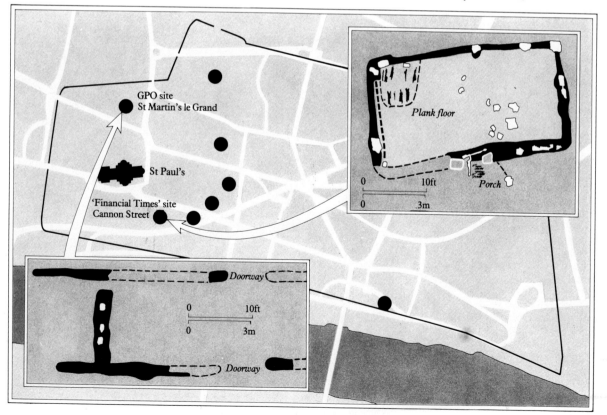

GPO site
St Martin's le Grand

St Paul's

'Financial Times' site
Cannon Street

Plank floor

0   10ft

0   3m

Porch

Doorway

0   10ft

0   3m

Doorway

Above: 'Trial-pieces' of bone and pottery (a scrap of Roman pottery): perhaps the attempts of apprentice metalworkers to master intricate patterns.

Below: Knife, from Putney, 10th-century; it is inlaid with a herring-bone pattern in silver and copper, and with a silver plate with the owner's name, 'Osmund'.

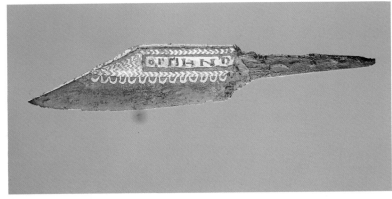

revenues. Royal decrees concerning London were addressed jointly to the portreeve and the bishop of London; they could be conveyed to the townspeople at their open-air assembly, the *folkmoot*, meeting beside St Paul's cathedral, where the affairs of the city were discussed. In Norman and later times London was divided into a number of *wards*, each administered by an *alderman*. The words are Anglo-Saxon, but it is not clear how early the system began.

The law-codes of the English kings were complex, but locally law-enforcement was left very much to private initiative. In the London area there was a *peace-gild*, a voluntary association of men of London, Middlesex and neighbouring areas for mutual aid, the pursuit of thieves and the compensation of their victims. This area may be 'the lands that belonged to' London in the days of King Edward, whose inhabitants had to supply labour for the upkeep of its walls and troops to defend it; London's influence already extended far beyond the city itself.

London's Buildings

The form of London's local government at this period may be obscure, but there is at least some archaeological evidence for the appearance of the city. Excavation has revealed traces of a number of domestic buildings of dates between the 9th and 11th centuries: a sunken-floored hut at Milk Street, similar buildings of different sizes, some of which may have had upper floors — the rectangular pit which is all the excavator finds having been a cellar — on a number of sites south of Cheapside, and a more substantial timber-framed hall near St Martin's le Grand. All were of timber; the ready supply of stone and brick from surviving ruins of Roman buildings was apparently ignored for domestic buildings.

Even some churches were of timber, though one reference to 'the old wooden church of St Andrew' (Holborn) in the 10th century perhaps implies that the fact that it was wooden was unusual and therefore notable. More churches were being built, some as the private chapels of London landowners for the use of their families, servants and tenants. All Hallows Gracechurch (Lombard Street) — 'Gracechurch' from its thatched roof

Above: **Rings and brooches, found in Cheapside, the unfinished stock of a London jeweller.**

Below left: **Highly decorated sword-pommel of silver-gilt, from Fetter Lane, Holborn.**

Below right: **Bronze mounts with traces of gilding, with the intricate interlace patterns of late Anglo-Saxon art, influenced by Scandinavian styles.**

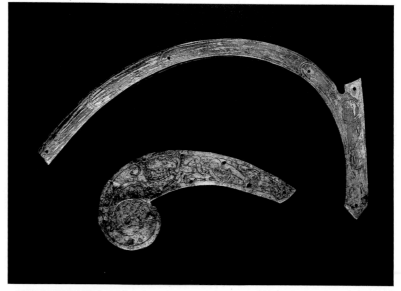

of 'grass' — seems to have been such a church; in the 1050s its owner and (probably) founder Brihtmaer gave it, with the right to appoint the priest and to collect tithes, to Canterbury Cathedral. These small city churches, of which none survive except as foundations — those of St Bride's (Fleet Street) can still be seen — could be highly ornamented and richly furnished; fragments of a decorated stone cross of the early 11th century preserved in the crypt of All Hallows by the Tower show the quality of religious sculpture of this time.

Trade and Industry

If London's medieval street-plan was already being formed in the days of King Alfred, its two main market streets, 'West Cheap' (the 'west market') or Cheapside, and East Cheap (the 'east market'), must have existed or been established at that time. The discovery of a stock of unfinished pewter jewellery in Cheapside may indicate that already by the 11th century Cheapside was a centre for the jewellers' and goldsmiths' crafts as it was in medieval and later times. The London goldsmiths were responsible for engraving the dies for the royal coinage, and supplying them to mints in other towns. Though little of their work in gold or silver survives, there are many examples of other decorative metalwork, much of it showing the influence of Scandinavian art, with extravagant interlace patterns of beasts and foliage; similar designs appear on more everyday items of bone and leather.

As well as local products the markets and wharves of London handled international trade. An English writer at the end of the 10th century, Aelfric, listed the exotic goods a merchant might carry: silks, precious stones, gold, wine, (olive) oil, ivory, bronze and glass and other luxuries. But a set of royal ordinances a little later mentions some of the more ordinary cargoes on which customs duty was payable at Billingsgate, one of London's chief wharves: planks, cloth, fish, chickens, eggs and dairy produce. Besides the local women dealing in cheese and butter (and paying two pence a year for the privilege) there were merchants from Flanders, Normandy, northern France and Germany. The foreign merchants were buying wool, which along with cloth was England's main export and source of wealth in the

middle ages; agricultural produce, fine embroidery and metalwork, and silver, usually in the form of coinage, were also exported.

Even before the wars of the 11th century placed a Danish king on the throne of England, the existence in the eastern half of the country of the Danelaw, largely Scandinavian in population, law and culture though ruled by the English king, encouraged links with the Scandinavian countries. The vikings who had terrorized northern Europe opened up trade routes along its coasts, and there were Scandinavian trading posts and settlements from the great rivers of Russia to Iceland, Greenland and, briefly, North America. London was in contact with this network of trade, and excavation produces Baltic amber, carvings in walrus-tusk ivory from the Arctic, even whetstones of a particularly suitable stone found only in southern Norway. In the other direction a pewter brooch has been found in Dublin which was made in the same mould as one in the group from Cheapside; the Cheapside jeweller clearly had contacts with the viking merchant town there. Most of the products of the north, such as fish, furs,

timber and rope, are not the sort of thing that survives well on archaeological sites. Nor do many of the luxuries from the south and east that Aelfric lists, though fragments of decorated glass vessels imported from Syria have been found.

It was the Thames that provided London's access to European trade. Ships with single square sails — the Billingsgate customs list refers to the larger vessels as *keels* and *hulks* — made the North Sea and Channel crossings and came upriver with the tide, while smaller river-craft carried local trade. Near Billingsgate excavation has revealed a timber and rubble platform laid down on which ships could be berthed; there were probably similiar arrangements elsewhere. The river-crossing — the earliest definite references to a bridge seem to be in the late 10th or early 11th century — made London a convenient place to tranship goods to or from land transport, and London's wharves would have been busy with ox-carts and pack-horses. But in the early 11th century the bridge and the wharves were also the objective of seafarers very different from the merchants of Scandinavia, France or Germany.

Above: **Bone comb carved at one end (originally both) with a stylized animal head.**

Below: **Carpenter's axe, found in an 11th-century pit at Milk Street. The handle is curved to keep the user's hand clear of his work.**

Danish and English Kings

New Danish Attacks

Towards the end of the 10th century a new series of attacks from Scandinavia began. The usual piratical raids quickly developed into a purposeful campaign to win back the Danelaw and gain political control over England. London was the focus of much of the fighting that followed. In 994 Swein, son of the king of Denmark, and the Norwegian Olaf Tryggvason led an attack on the city, which held out with a determination that surprised the attackers. Over the next 20 years London was attacked time and time again; 'but praise God, still it stands safe and sound', an English chronicler commented in 1009. Fighting centred around the wharves and the bridge which barred the river. A later Icelandic historian recorded an attack in which Olaf (who changed sides after 994) destroyed the bridge, though the obscure poem that inspired his account seems to describe an attack on the 'wharf' rather than the 'bridge' of London. Certainly the Dane Cnut found the bridge so well defended in 1016 that he was forced to drag his ships around it along a channel dug through low-lying ground at its southern end, before he could lay siege to the city.

By the end of 1016 the English king Aethelred and his eldest son Edmund were dead, as was Swein. The Londoners had already made a separate peace with the new Danish leader, Cnut, and he was accepted as king of all England. During the wars the invaders had often been bought off by payments of *danegeld*; similar payments continued, converted into a regular tax to pay for a standing army and fleet. Something of London's wealth is indicated by the fact that in 1018 the city was taxed the huge sum of 10,500 pounds in silver — nearly 5 tons of silver pennies or bullion — to pay off Cnut's seamen.

Edward the Confessor

For some 25 years Cnut's family ruled England. Many of his court were of course of Scandinavian origin, and there

Fleet of viking ships, scratched on a piece of wood by a medieval idler in the Norwegian port of Bergen.

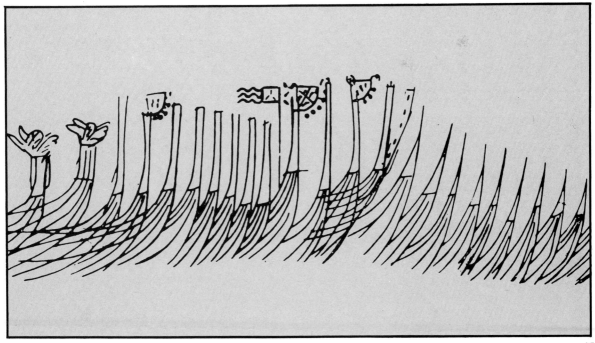

Above: **Viking battle-axes and spears from the Thames at London Bridge: the result of a battle, or thrown into the river as an offering to the gods?**

Below: **Stone slab from a monumental tomb erected at St Paul's, perhaps for a member of the court of the Danish King Cnut. It is carved with an inscription in the Norse runic alphabet.**

was strong Scandinavian influence on England, on its law, its language, its culture and its art. But in June 1042 King Harthacnut, Cnut's son, died suddenly 'as he stood at his drink' at a wedding-feast in Lambeth. He had no son to succeed him, and by popular decision the crown was offered to Edward, surviving son of the former English king Aethelred.

Edward had spent much of his life in exile in Normandy at the court of the Dukes Richard (his uncle) and Robert (his cousin). Nicknamed 'the Confessor' ('the priest'), he was a man of great piety. In his later years he devoted much of his energy and much of the royal income to the building, on an island in the marshy mouth of the river Tyburn where it entered the Thames 1½ miles (2km) west of London, of a new abbey dedicated to St Peter — Westminster, the 'west monastery'. There had long been a church here, perhaps from the days of King Offa of Mercia, and a small community of monks, while just to the north, in what is now Whitehall, excavation has revealed a hall and a farmstead of the 9th or 10th century. Edward reorganized the monastery, granting it large new estates, and had a great church built, in the style of the churches he had seen in Normandy.

Next to the abbey Edward built himself a hall. If earlier kings had indeed had a palace in the north-west corner of the city of London, Edward abandoned it. At Westminster he had his palace and his royal church — the abbey: a royal centre separate from the busy commercial city. He thus paved the way for the dual development of London and Westminster as mercantile and administrative capitals — though this development was many years in the future.

Just after Christmas 1065 the abbey church was consecrated; a week later Edward was dead. He was buried in his new church, where his tomb became a shrine and a place of pilgrimage. He left an unsettled kingdom. He had no heir, and had apparently promised the throne both to the Norman Duke William and to the English Earl Harold of Wessex, who had governed much of England on his behalf for 10 years; meanwhile the Scandinavians awaited the opportunity to launch a new invasion.

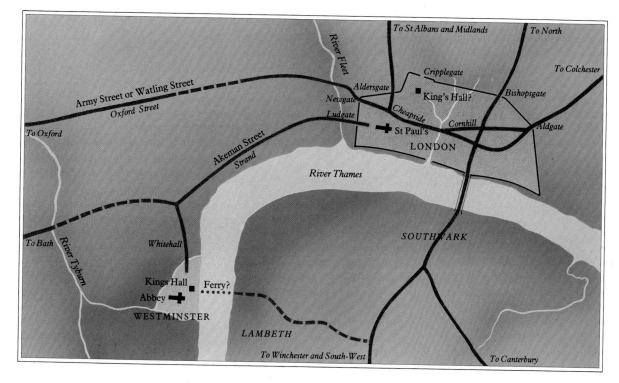

Above: London and Westminster: the
siting of Edward the Confessor's new
palace.

Below: The consecration of
Westminster Abbey and the funeral of
King Edward, as shown on the
11th-century Bayeux Tapestry.

The Normans

Above: **After their defeat near Hastings the English flee from the pursuing Normans, leaving their dead on the field (Bayeux Tapestry).**

Below: **William I. The formalized portrait of the king, with crown and sceptre, on a silver penny.**

1066

The English leaders quickly elected Earl Harold as king, initiating the catastrophic events of the year 1066. In September Harold led the English to victory over an invading Norwegian force in Yorkshire, only to learn that William of Normandy had landed with his army on the south coast. Once more, as in the days of Alfred, the men of London marched out with the king's forces to meet the invader. This time, on 14th October near Hastings, they were defeated, their king killed. The English retreated on London, which they hoped to hold. William's advance was slow. He was wary of the well-defended city, particularly after his vanguard was driven back from the south end of the bridge, and led his troops in a wide loop round to the west, cutting London off. At last at Berkhamsted (Herts.) the English surrendered; among the English nobles who offered William the throne were 'all the best men from London'. On Christmas Day at Westminster Abbey William was crowned king.

William and London

After his coronation William built castles in London 'against the restlessness of the large and fierce populace'. One of these was probably Baynard's Castle, on the west of the city, just south of Ludgate, where with an adjacent castle, the Tower of Montfichet, it could control the road to Westminster and the precinct of St Paul's, the symbolic centre of the city. A better-known, and longer-lived, castle was also probably first built at this time, in the south-east corner of the city, where the Roman city wall provided defence on the east and on the river-side, requiring only an earth rampart and a ditch to cut off the angle. Soon, before 1080, work began on a more substantial structure

William I's charter to the citizens of London.

within this enclosure, a fortified palace of stone, the White Tower. Gradually over the next 200 years the walled area around it was extended, creating the great concentric fortress, the Tower of London, that stands today.

In charge of London, as portreeve, William placed one of his leading supporters, Geoffrey de Mandeville, who may have governed the city from the Tower. But the Norman king's attitude to London was not wholly one of repression. An early document addressed to the portreeve Geoffrey — jointly with the bishop of London as in Anglo-Saxon days — was a 'charter', a formal letter from the king, guaranteeing the citizens' rights:

'William the king greets William the bishop and Geoffrey the portreeve and all the citizens in London, French and English, in friendship. I inform you that I intend you to have all the rights in law you had in the days of King Edward, and each child to be his father's heir after his father's day; and I will not allow any man to do you any wrong. God keep you.'

Friendly in tone, though perhaps vague as to the privileges it offers, it confirms that there would be no further confiscation of property. It demonstrates the caution with which William approached his wealthiest and most populous town and the care he was willing to take to conciliate its citizens.

Westminster and Domesday Book

In spite of the building of the new castles, London's royal centre remained at Westminster, and in 1097-99 a new hall was built there to replace that of Edward the Confessor. It was very large, about 240 feet (75m) long, with stone walls and a wooden roof probably supported on two rows of columns; with a new grander roof added in the 1390s it survives today.

But like their Anglo-Saxon predecessors the early Norman kings had no single capital. It was from Gloucester that in 1085 William issued orders for a survey of his kingdom, and to Winchester, the old West Saxon royal city, close rival to London as meeting-place of the royal court, that the returns came in the following year. From this survey two volumes were compiled, the 'Domesday Book', a register of landholders, of rents and of the economic potential, largely agricultural, of each estate. From it can be derived a picture of the economic geography of 11th-century England: an essentially rural country with a population around 1½ million, the towns rather anomalies, few with more than 2,000 inhabitants. The Domesday statistics for the countryside were recorded systematically; the complex organization of a town seems largely to

The Tower of London, *c*. 1100. Recent excavations have shown that this reconstruction model is incorrect in some details; the riverside was fortified not as shown here by a wooden stockade but by a still-standing Roman stone wall.

Above: The chapel of St John in the White Tower, late 11th-century, one of the finest surviving examples of early Norman architecture in England.

Below: As originally built by William II Westminster Hall had an arcade and a series of round-headed windows high up in the side walls.

have defeated the surveyors. London and Winchester were omitted, except for incidental references, and one can only guess that the population of London was 10-12,000 at this time. For the city we hear only of the properties there owned by rural estates — the 28 houses paying 13s 8½d rent to Barking Abbey, for example, or the 46 burgesses worth 40s a year to Staines. As well as rental income such properties provided a country landowner with access to London's markets and a town residence if he had business at the king's court.

Unhelpful as far as the city is concerned, the Domesday survey of the neighbouring counties gives a much clearer picture of the countryside around. Such places as 'Stibenhede' (Stepney) and 'Chenesitun' (Kensington) were already well-established villages with ploughland, woods and grazing for cattle and pigs, while riverside settlements like 'Fuleham' had fisheries. Surplus produce must have found its way to London for sale, for the merchants and craftsmen of the city had to look beyond it for their food.

The Church

Cathedral and Parish Churches

In 1087 one of the many fires from which London suffered destroyed St Paul's Cathedral. The original church of 604 would have undergone much extension and rebuilding in the Saxon period — there had been at least one earlier fire and subsequent rebuilding, in 962; nothing is known of the shape or size of the church that perished in 1087. Rebuilding quickly began, aided by royal patronage, but was to drag on for many years. There was another fire in the 1130s, which delayed the work, but by 1148 the eastern arm, the choir, which probably had an apsidal end, was complete. Work on the western arm (the nave) and the north and south transepts continued; for over 50 years these must have had temporary wooden roofs, for their stone vaulting was not completed until early in the 13th century, as was the central tower with its great lead-clad timber spire rising about 450 feet (140m) above the city. Even now (1980) only two buildings in London exceed this height — the Post Office Tower and the National Westminster Bank building — though the City's Barbican towers approach it. In 1256 work began to extend the choir eastwards and remodel it in the new Gothic style; the enlarged church, one of the finest of English cathedrals, survived until the Great Fire of 1666.

As the spire of St Paul's dominated early pictures of London the cathedral dominated much of city life. The precinct around it contained church buildings, the bishop's palace, and according to later tradition the meeting

Bronze hanging lamp, from St Martin's le Grand. This lamp, which burnt oil, may have hung over the altar of the monastic church of St Martin's.

Right: St Paul's cathedral. An engraving, made shortly before the destruction of the medieval cathedral in the Great Fire of 1666, shows the view eastwards along the magnificent Norman nave.

Below: St John's, Clerkenwell. The vaulted crypt of the church of the Knights of St John, begun in the 1140s.

place of the folkmoot. The figure of St Paul appeared on the city's seal in the 13th century, and, according to one description, on the banner which the men of London carried into battle. The bishop and the cathedral authorities owned property all over the city and large estates in Middlesex (Stepney, Willesden and Fulham, for example) and around, including the castle and town of Bishop's Stortford (Herts.).

Writing in about 1180 William Fitz Stephen reckoned that besides St Paul's there were in the city and its suburbs 13 monastic churches and 126 parish churches. Medieval statistics are notoriously unreliable, and it is difficult to define the area of the 'suburbs' in such a way that these figures are accurate. Certainly by William Fitz Stephen's time there were about 100 parish churches within the city wall. They were small, most serving a small community of neighbours, the parish boundary defined by the back walls of their properties.

Some were clearly founded by a landlord for the use of his family and tenants; some, like St Mary Woolnoth (Wulfnoth), bear their founder's name as an addition to that of the saint. In the 12th century, a time of church reformation and reorganization, these private churches, where the owner himself appointed the priest, tended to pass into the hands of cathedral or monastic authorities. In contrast to the tiny parishes in the central area of the city were larger ones on the outskirts, where the population was less dense.

Monasteries and Hospitals

An important feature of the medieval church, and one that was increasing in importance in the 11th and 12th centuries, was the monastic system; closed communities of men or women living a religious life according to a rule or order, free of responsibilities to a parish, but sometimes carrying out other spiritual or social duties for the benefit of people at large. The 13 monastic houses that William Fitz Stephen counted must have included two founded before the Norman conquest: the Abbey of St Peter (Westminster), which under royal favour, the chosen place of coronation of all the kings from Harold and William I on, was growing immensely in wealth and importance; and St Martin's le Grand, inside the city wall near Aldersgate, perhaps built on land released when the royal palace was trans-

ferred to Westminster — not large, but important as a sanctuary, an island within the city not subject to the legal control of the civic authorities. Others were set up in the late 11th and the 12th centuries on open land on the edge of the city and in the countryside around: at Bermondsey in 1089, at St Mary Overy, Southwark, at Holy Trinity, Aldgate — founded by Matilda, wife of Henry I, in 1108, and supported by some of the most important men of London — and at St Bartholomew, Smithfield. Early in the 12th century a nunnery was founded at Holywell, Shoreditch, and another, dedicated to St Mary, at Clerkenwell.

Next to St Mary's Clerkenwell stood the Priory of St John, founded by the Knights Hospitallers; the similar and rival order of Knights Templars established their English headquarters near Holborn in 1128, later moving to a new site by the river, where their church, with a circular nave in imitation of the Church of the Holy Sepulchre in Jerusalem, still stands. These two military orders were founded to win back the Holy Land from the Saracens and to guard the pilgrim routes. The Templars, an extremely wealthy order, were noted as bankers and financiers; their London precinct housed a royal treasury for many years.

Perhaps a more appropriate service provided by the church was the care of the sick and the needy. 'Hospitals', some to house the sick, some as refuges for the poor or hostels for travellers, were established under ecclesiastical control. Royalty, nobles and townsfolk made donations and bequests for their upkeep and for the good of their own souls. Little medical treatment was given; the care rather than the cure of the sick was their function. Of the hospitals that of St Bartholomew, adjacent to the priory, was the best-known and longest surviving. A special group of hospitals were those which housed lepers. Two 11th-century bishops of London had died of leprosy, a disease known and feared throughout Europe. Sufferers were outcasts, driven from towns, forced to beg for their food. Around London a ring of leper hospitals grew up as refuges for lepers driven out of the city or passing along the main roads. The first one was that at St Giles' (Bloomsbury), founded and endowed by Queen Matilda. Her example of charity was followed by many others.

Wealth and Trade

Left: Foreign pottery imported into London in the 11th–12th centuries included grey-ware 'ladles' and pots with painted decoration from the Rhineland and glazed vessels like this spouted pitcher from what is now Belgium.

Right: The crypt of the Prior of Lewes' house (formerly the Earl de Warenne's), Southwark.

Merchants and Immigrants

If William Fitz Stephen's estimate of the number of churches in 12th-century London is unreliable, modern estimates of its *population* are more so. The population, however, may have grown to around 20,000 by the end of the century, including an increasing number of foreign immigrants and transient visitors. Merchants from Rouen had already been trading in London before the Norman conquest, but further settlers from the Norman kings' French domains followed the invaders. 'Many natives of the chief Norman cities, Rouen and Caen', as a 12th-century writer explains, 'settled in London as the foremost town in England, because it was more suited to commerce and better stored with the goods in which they were accustomed to trade'. German traders had long travelled the routes linking Thames and Rhine, and in the 12th century the 'men of Cologne' had a 'house' or 'guildhall' by the Thames, their permanent London headquarters and trading-post.

Among other business men attracted to London were Jews. The first Jewish settlers seem to have come from Rouen, where a long-established Jewish colony had been attacked and many Jews killed in 1096. Forbidden by Christian law from themselves engaging in trade or industry they provided financial backing for others. They acted as money-lenders to merchants, nobles and kings, so obtaining grudging royal protection. By 1130 there was a London community led by Rabbi Joseph, centred on 'Jews' Street' (Old Jewry). Until 1177, although there were Jewish residents in many English towns, only in London were they allowed a cemetery, outside Cripplegate, to which all Jews who died in England were brought for burial. Jews remained aliens, not integrated into English society. Kings were ever eager to find excuses to extort money from them,

while they attracted the envy, sometimes the fear, of their Christian neighbours — who might well be in debt to them. In 1189 an incident at the coronation of Richard I sparked off a riot in which the London Jewry was burnt and 30 Jews were killed. Similar violence occurred elsewhere, and Jews were never safe from extortion and intimidation.

Town Houses

During the events of 1189 Jews took refuge in their stone houses in the Jewry. Other wealthy merchants must have had similar houses; stone houses in Cheapside are mentioned in building-

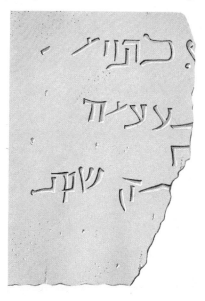

regulations of 1212, and their remains have been found elsewhere in the city. They probably resembled surviving examples in Lincoln, Southampton and other towns: simple rectangular buildings with a hall — the living accommodation — on the upper floor reached by an outside staircase, a shop or warehouse below.

Most buildings, however, were of timber, like those of earlier times, with a roof of thatch. Fires could start easily and spread rapidly; in a fire in (probably) 1133 much of the city from Aldgate to St Paul's was burnt down. Though buildings were close enough together for fire to spread there were still large open areas within the city walls; but suburbs were growing up in Southwark and along the road to Westminster. According to William Fitz Stephen 'almost all the bishops, abbots and nobles of England are, as it were, citizens and townsmen of London, having their fine houses there . . .' Such men had country estates, but used their town houses when in London on business. Much larger than the houses of city merchants, these establishments would have a separate main hall, perhaps a chapel, a kitchen, accommodation for servants, stables and store-sheds. Such a house was that in Southwark which was later acquired by the Prior of Lewes,

Left: Fragment of a Jewish tombstone, commemorating 'Nahum': found in 1753 built into the medieval city wall, where it had been used for repairs, but since lost.

though it was built in the 12th century perhaps for the Earl de Warenne. The fine stone-vaulted cellar that lay under the hall of this house survived until it was demolished in connection with road-works in the 1830s.

The River and the Bridge

The Earl de Warenne's house was conveniently situated near the south end of London Bridge. The bridge was essential to London's existence, the only bridge across the lower Thames. The river had been bridged at just about this point by the Romans; how long the Roman bridge lasted and what attempts the Saxons made to repair or replace it are not clear — it may have been superseded by a ferry for some time. Certainly by the early 11th century a bridge existed, a barrier to enemy fleets and a convenient place for collecting tolls on shipping. The bridge was of wood, prone to continual damage by flood, frost and fire, and in 1176 work began on a stouter bridge of stone. A quarter of a mile long, on 19 piers with a drawbridge to allow larger ships through, it was one of the earliest stone bridges in medieval Europe, a wonder commented on by all later visitors to London. The work, which continued for many years, was encouraged by King John and backed by Londoners' donations. Bequests of land of which the rents could go towards the costs of the bridge, and the income from houses and shops built on the bridge itself, paid for its upkeep. 'Old London Bridge' survived, much altered and repaired, until 1830.

Both up- and downstream of the bridge wharves were stretching along the north bank of the river. There was a piecemeal development of private quays, already beginning in places in the 11th century; each landowner extended his property southwards by erecting embankments or timber revetments to reclaim the fore-shore and to provide moorings for new larger ships. Smaller vessels carried considerable local trade upriver and on tributaries such as the Lea and Medway. There were complaints that this traffic was being obstructed by dams built across the rivers to provide power for watermills and by fixed fish-traps, complaints that led to royal procla-mations in 1197 and 1199 ordering the destruction of such weirs — probably, like most such proclamations, to little effect.

Above: **Wicker-lined pit with cross-timbers, probably used for some industrial function in the 12th century, behind houses in Milk Street.**

Below: **The demolition of one of the piers of Old London Bridge in 1826 showed how it was constructed on a foundation of rubble held in place by timber piles.**

The Barons of London

The Common Seal of London. The early 13th-century seal shows St Paul and is inscribed in Latin 'Seal of the barons of London'.

City Government

Richard I's proclamation in 1197 against the obstruction of the Thames was issued 'for the common good of our city of London'. It was presumably made at the request — and probably the expense — of Londoners, users of the river. During the 12th century the influence of London's citizens and their ability to organize themselves developed considerably. They were able to buy or extort privileges from kings, privileges embodied in a series of royal charters still preserved in the Corporation of London's Records Office. These documents are often obscure, and the steps by which during the century London achieved a considerable degree of self-government are not clear. Royal communications were no longer addressed to the portreeve; the title *sheriff* ('shire-reeve', the king's representative in a shire or county) was adopted. We hear of *two* sheriffs, of London and Middlesex; for a while there appeared another official, the *justiciar*, apparently

responsible for the administration of royal justice in the city. Londoners won the right to choose their own sheriffs for the city and Middlesex rather than accepting the king's appointments; for this privilege they paid an inclusive sum of £300 each year to the royal treasury in place of piecemeal tax assessments.

The folkmoot continued to meet by St Paul's, but the complex business of administering a populous city, filled with newcomers from other parts of the king's territory, English and French, and with foreign merchants, quickly exceeded the scope of any large open meeting. Administration passed into the hands of a more select assembly of chief citizens, who acquired the title *aldermen* ('elders'), a title reserved under the Anglo-Saxon kings for their leading subjects. By the end of the century they were probably already meeting regularly in a building on the site of the later Guildhall.

Their assembly was the *husting*. This court — the derivation of its name from Old Norse ('house-meeting') suggests Scandinavian influence — seems to have been ruling on standard weights and measures already in the 10th century, and continued this interest in trade and the relations between merchants; its members were themselves drawn from the wealthy merchant class.

In time of war the aldermen organized the city's defence; in time of peace they administered its law. By the early 12th century the city was divided into areas, *wards*, each governed by an alderman; the system perhaps had its beginning much earlier. Some of these wards may have originated in the areas of private jurisdiction over their tenants that certain large landowners held within the

city. Certainly an alderman's power was personal, not conferred by election to an office. Wards were named after their aldermen, and there was a tendency for the position to remain within a family. Within his ward the alderman had considerable authority, and held his own law-court, the *wardmoot*.

The Barons and the Mayor

The aldermen were a merchant oligarchy, the leading members of a community which was referred to in documents of the period as 'the barons of London'. The term seems to mean those inhabitants of London who had full legal privileges and liabilities, those of status to be represented in negotiations with the king or his councillors. The commercial towns of Normandy, such as Rouen, from which some of London's merchant families came, had long had a measure of independence from royal or ducal control and were organized as self-governing communities to which the name *communes* was applied. Not surprisingly the 'barons' of London sought similar status for their own town. Kings were not eager to accept such an innovation, and it was not until 1191 that Richard I formally recognized the existence of the Londoners' own 'commune'. Henceforth London was treated as a single community, not a group of individuals.

A French commune appointed its own chief magistrate, its *mayor*. Londoners would not be satisfied with the right merely of choosing the royal sheriffs, with such a model before them. They unofficially adopted the title 'mayor' for their chosen leader before they received royal authorization. A document of 1193 is 'the Oath of the Commune' — to keep faith to King Richard, to preserve the commune, and to obey the mayor. King

John refers in a charter to 'our mayor and citizens', but it was not until 1215 that he formally gave permission for his barons of London to choose themselves a mayor each year 'faithful, discreet and fit to govern the city'.

The Gilds

Alongside the mayor, the aldermen and their court, other institutions were developing in this period that would be equally important in the administration of the medieval city. London's 'peace-gild' in the 10th century had been one of the many *gilds* in late Saxon England — sworn associations of individuals with common interests. In return for a regular subscription (the word *gild* simply means 'payment') they provided their members with support in time of trouble, collective religious ceremonies and, perhaps most attractive, regular feasting. In towns, amidst a large floating population, they supplied a sense of security; they were established bodies to which a man could turn for the sort of help which in more stable rural communities he could expect from family, neighbours or feudal landlord. For many townsmen their common interests were with others in the same trade; so already by 1130 there was a gild of weavers in London. Other gilds had social or charitable functions. In 1179/80 a number were listed which had been set up without the king's approval; they included several 'of the bridge', which presumably devoted their funds to work on the new stone bridge. But some had trade or craft titles — goldsmiths, pepperers, butchers — and it is these, like the weavers' gild, which, although they were not the direct ancestors of any of the gilds or companies which in later medieval times controlled London's trade and industry, foreshadowed their development.

Thus Anglo-Saxon aldermen and gilds, Scandinavian husting and Norman-French commune and mayor came together in the 12th century to form the basic structure of London's future government.

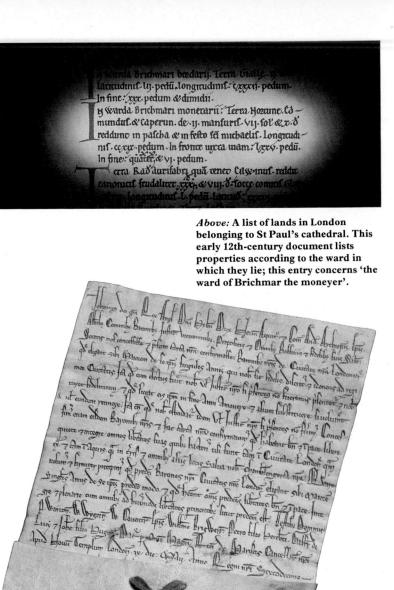

Above: **A list of lands in London belonging to St Paul's cathedral. This early 12th-century document lists properties according to the ward in which they lie; this entry concerns 'the ward of Brichmar the moneyer'.**

Charter of King John, 9th May 1215. Issued by the king a few weeks before the Magna Carta, this document grants Londoners the right to elect a mayor each year.

'Most Noble City'

Above: **Common Seal. On the opposite face to the figure of St Paul was that of St Thomas Becket, enthroned over the London skyline.**

Left: **William Fitz Stephen's description of London: the opening of a copy of the 12th-century description included in a 14th-century book of City laws and customs.**

One of London's portreeves in the early 12th century was Gilbert Becket, a merchant from Rouen who, like others, had established himself as a leading citizen of London. His son Thomas, born and brought up in London, became Chancellor of England and archbishop of Canterbury, and, until their fatal argument over the relationship of church and state, a close friend and confidant of King Henry II. On 29th December 1170 Archbishop Thomas was murdered in Canterbury Cathedral by a group of knights acting, they believed, on the wishes of the king. Three years later he was canonized as a saint and martyr. In official documents he had called himself 'Thomas of London', and London quickly adopted the new saint as a patron. His image, clad in his archbishop's robes,

29

was placed on one side of the city's seal, with the short Latin verse, a prayer:

ME QUE TE PEPERI
NE CESSES THOMA TUERI

'May you not cease, Thomas, to protect me, (the city) that bore you'.

The chapel on the new stone bridge was dedicated to St Thomas; later a hospital was founded on the site of his birthplace in Cheapside.

Among the eye-witnesses of Thomas' murder was his secretary, William Fitz Stephen ('William son of Stephen'), a fellow Londoner who had worked with him for many years. Some time later William wrote an account of the saint's life. To a London reader it is his preface, in which he describes London itself, the saint's birthplace, which is most interesting. William wrote in Latin, like all his contemporaries, and his delight in obscure Latin words, flowery phrases, and apt quotations from Roman authors, was matched only by his enthusiasm for his home town, 'the most noble city'. To William it was the best of all possible towns, spoilt only by 'the immoderate drinking of fools and the frequency of fires'. Neither archaeology nor history can provide confirmation of the former complaint; for the latter there is plenty of evidence in chronicle accounts of the many great fires of the 11th and 12th centuries, and in early 13th-century attempts to encourage the building of more fire-proof houses. The picture William presents is idealized, but it remains the earliest description of the town by someone who knew it well.

William begins: 'Among the noble cities of the world which Fame celebrates, the city of London, seat of the monarchy of England, is the one which spreads its

Above right: **Pilgrim's *ampulla*. This container for holy water was brought back to London by a 13th-century visitor to the shrine of St Thomas at Canterbury. On it is a scene of Thomas' murder.**

Bottom right: **The riverside wall. Excavation shows how, just as William Fitz Stephen described, the Roman wall had been eroded by the Thames. Broken stonework lies on top of the dark river silts which undermine the wall.**

Left: **12th-century horseshoes. Horses sold at the weekly market at Smithfield were essential in war and for transport and haulage.**

Below: **Bone skates, their undersides polished by the use on the ice. Found in the Moorfields area, they are of the type described by William Fitz Stephen.**

fame more widely, distributes its goods and merchandise further and holds its head higher.' He proceeds to describe the advantages of London's situation and its climate and the innate virtue of its citizens. Its Christian faith is evident, he thinks, in the number of churches — the 13 great monastic houses and the 126 parish churches.

William describes the city's fortifications. There was the 'palatine fortress' (the Tower) in the east, two other castles in the west. On the north was the city wall with towers and seven 'doubled' gates. The wall and its towers remained much as they were when built by the Romans. Defensive works of some sort had been carried out in the days of King Alfred, but only minor piecemeal repairs and improvements seem to have been undertaken on the wall and its defensive ditch before the 13th century. The gates (does William mean they had twin arches?) were presumably patched-up Roman structures, though one, Aldgate, was rebuilt early in the 12th century, while another must at least have been extensively altered to justify the name 'Newgate' which it bore already in the

1180s. On the riverside, as William says and archaeology proves, the Roman wall had been eroded by 'the fishy River Thames'. Beyond the walls lay an area of fields, pastures and woodland with streams and clear springs, where Londoners strolled on summer evenings. To the west, at Westminster, stood the royal palace 'an incomparable building', joined to the city by a pleasant suburb. Though William describes London as 'the seat of the monarchy' the idea of a political capital was to come only much later. Yet the Exchequer, the department set up in the 12th century to handle the kingdom's finances, was soon based at Westminster — even though the royal treasury was at Winchester. William's statement may have been a slight exaggeration in his own day, but it fore-shadowed reality.

His enthusiastic description of the schools attached to the city's chief churches — the pupils' Latin exercises as well as the cockfights they held, apparently in the schoolroom, on Shrove Tuesday — must reflect his own boy-hood; 'for we were all boys once'. He is equally enthusiastic about the cookshop

by the river, in the area where the winetrade was carried on (the Vintry). Here you could buy ready-cooked meals to satisfy even the most choosy of unexpected guests.

Tradesmen and craftsmen, he says, had their own quarters where they worked and sold their wares. This localization of particular shops and industries is a feature of London's topography throughout the middle ages, and is reflected in many of the city's street-names, such as Bread Street, Milk Street and Ironmonger Lane. One market he describes in some detail: the weekly horse and cattle fair held on the 'smooth field' (West Smithfield — ancestor of the present meat market), with its impromptu horse-races to show off the animals' speed.

William turns to verse to describe London's international trade:

The Arab sends gold, the Sabaean spice and incense,
The Scythian weapons; the fertile land of Babylon
Sends palm-oil from its rich forests, the Nile its precious stones;
The Chinese send purple-dyed cloths, the French their wines,
The Norwegians and Russians send squirrel fur, miniver and sables.

His list sounds fanciful, but documents and archaeology agree that highly valuable imports from such exotic places were indeed reaching London in the 12th century.

London, says William, is considerably older than Rome. At first sight merely another fanciful claim, in fact it reflects the belief of medieval writers that Britain had first been colonized by a group of exiled Trojans, and that on the site of London they had founded a city called New Troy. New Troy or *Trinovantum* was the invention of Geoffrey of Monmouth, a historian writing some 40 years before, who was unscrupulous in the use of historical sources and imaginative embroidery upon them; it was eagerly taken up by such writers as William, for it provided London with a pedigree to match its contemporary status. It constituted for William the basis for a favourable comparison of London with ancient Rome, for since the legendary founders of that city also were of Trojan stock the same laws, he believed, applied in each city!

From the city's origins and institutions William turns to its pleasures and pastimes: 'it is not good for a city only to be busy and serious unless it is also pleasant and merry'. He describes Shrove Tuesday football, jousting in Lent, regattas on the Thames at Easter, athletics and dancing in the summer, the baiting of boars, bulls and bears in winter. He devotes special attention to winter-sports, when the marsh (the Moor or Moorfields) outside the walls to the north is frozen: 'there are others more skilful at playing on the ice' who tie the shinbones of animals to their feet as skates and push themselves along with iron-spiked sticks 'as fast as a flying bird or javelin from a catapult'. Hunting with hawk and hound in the woods around London was popular: 'the citizens have the right to hunt in Middlesex, Hertfordshire, the whole of the Chilterns, and Kent as far as the River Cray' — an unusual privilege in an England whose kings were jealous of their own hunting-rights, but one which the citizens certainly claimed in the 1130s as an age-old custom, and which perhaps was given royal confirmation.

William concludes by stating that the city has produced many famous men, one of them being 'the Blessed Thomas, the archbishop, Christ's glorious martyr'. Anyone interested in London's past must be equally glad that the city produced William Fitz Stephen. He was not a great writer, but his range of quotations from classical authors shows him to be well-read, a credit to the London school where he was educated. He provides a lively picture of the city to set beside the workaday evidence of archaeology and documents. If he overlooked London's imperfections in his enthusiasm he was not the last Londoner to do so. London, 'lucky in the healthfulness of its climate, in its Christian faith, in the strength of its defences, the nature of its site, the honour of its citizens, the chastity of its women', has attracted others to praise it, others to condemn it.

'CERTAINLY A GOOD CITY, WHEN IT HAS A GOOD LORD!'

Books to Read

T. Baker
Medieval London, Cassell 1970

M. Biddle and D. Hudson
The Future of London's Past, 'Rescue' 1973

C.N.L. Brooke and G. Keir
London 800-1216: the shaping of a city, Secker and Warburg 1975

N. Pevsner (revised by B. Cherry)
The Buildings of England: London, (2 vols.) Penguin 1973/1952

C. Platt
The English Medieval Town, Secker and Warburg 1976

F.M. Stenton
'Norman London' in D.M. Stenton (ed.)
Preparatory to Anglo-Saxon England, OUP 1970

John Stow
Survey of London, Everyman (revised ed.) 1956

London Museum Catalogues
(R.E.M. Wheeler)
No.1 London and the Vikings, 1927
No.6 London and the Saxons, 1936

Museum of London, Dept. of Urban Archaeology
Archaeology of the City of London, City of London Archaeological Trust 1980

As this list indicates, very few books are available on London in this period, particularly the earlier part of it, though it receives some attention in the more general works listed. John Stow's *Survey,* first published in 1598, is included because it incorporates the full text of William Fitz Stephen's description of London in the 1170s; the Everyman edition contains an English translation of William's Latin. In addition to the account of the recent work of the Museum of London's own Department of Urban Archaeology listed here, more detailed reports on excavations in the London area by this and other units appear in the magazines *The London Archaeologist* and *Current Archaeology,* and in the *Transactions* and *Special Papers* published by the London and Middlesex Archaeological Society.

Places to Visit

MUSEUMS
The Museum of London: Saxon and medieval galleries
British Museum: Anglo-Saxon and medieval galleries; coin gallery
Public Record Office Museum: Domesday Book

Other smaller museums in the London area, such as **Kingston-upon-Thames Museum and Art Gallery,** contain some material of this period. Opening times can be found in *Museums and Galleries* (ABC Historic Publications, annually).

BUILDINGS
Very few buildings of this period survive in London. Further information on those listed, and others, will be found in the appropriate volumes in the Penguin *Buildings of England* series. Not all are generally open to visitors; in particular churches in urban areas, regrettably, cannot be left unlocked and unguarded, and application for access may have to be made locally — though churches in the City are normally open on weekdays. Archaeological excavations in London are sometimes open to the public; information on current excavations can be obtained from the Museum of London.

CENTRAL LONDON:
All Hallows by the Tower, Tower Hill: Saxon arch, cross fragments
City wall, Cooper's Row: ?12th-century rebuilding
St Bartholomew the Great, Smithfield: largely early 12th-century
St Bride's, Fleet Street: in crypt, foundations of Saxon and medieval church
St John's, Clerkenwell: 12th-century crypt
St Mary-le-Bow, Cheapside: late 11th-century crypt
Temple Church, Fleet Street: late 12th-century nave and porch
Tower of London: White Tower, late 11th-century; Bell Tower and parts of wall, late 12th - 13th-century
Westminster Abbey: late 11th-century Pyx Chapel and undercroft
Westminster Hall: late 11th-century, with later roof

OUTER LONDON AND BEYOND:
A number of former village churches now swallowed up by the spread of London's suburbs are Norman or contain Norman work, for example:
East Ham (St Mary's): 12th-century with 16th-century tower
Harlington, Middlesex (St Peter and St Paul): nave and doorway
Harmondsworth, Middlesex (St Mary's): south aisle and doorway

Further out are the Norman abbeys at **Waltham Abbey, Essex,** and **St Albans, Herts.** At **Rochester, Kent,** are the castle and cathedral; there are other castles at **Berkhamsted, Herts** and **Windsor, Berks** and the unique Saxon wooden church at **Greensted,** near **Ongar, Essex.**